DATE DUE   MAR   2013

976.1
Ala

Alabama : the Heart of Dixie

A Guide to AMERICAN STATES

Alabama

THE HEART OF DIXIE

MEDIA ENHANCED BOOKS
AV2 BY WEIGL
ADDED VALUE • AUDIO VISUAL

www.av2books.com

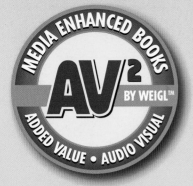

AV² provides enriched content that supplements and complements this book. Weigl's AV² books strive to create inspired learning and engage young minds in a total learning experience.

Your AV² Media Enhanced books come alive with...

Audio
Listen to sections of the book read aloud.

Key Words
Study vocabulary, and complete a matching word activity.

Go to **www.av2books.com**, and enter this book's unique code.

Video
Watch informative video clips.

Quizzes
Test your knowledge.

BOOK CODE

G 2 3 9 7 6 4

Embedded Weblinks
Gain additional information for research.

Slide Show
View images and captions, and prepare a presentation.

AV² by Weigl brings you media enhanced books that support active learning.

Try This!
Complete activities and hands-on experiments.

... and much, much more!

Published by AV² by Weigl
350 5th Avenue, 59th Floor
New York, NY 10118
Website: www.av2books.com   www.weigl.com

Library of Congress Cataloging-in-Publication Data

Parker, Janice.
 Alabama / Janice Parker.
   p. cm. -- (A guide to American states)
 Includes index.
 ISBN 978-1-61690-773-0 (hardcover : alk. paper) -- ISBN 978-1-61690-448-7 (online)
 1. Alabama--Juvenile literature. I. Title.
 F326.3.P373 2011
 976.1--dc22
                          2011018312

Printed in the United States of America in North Mankato, Minnesota

052011
WEP180511

Project Coordinator Jordan McGill
Art Director Terry Paulhus

Photo Credits
Every reasonable effort has been made to trace ownership and to obtain permission to reprint copyright material. The publishers would be pleased to have any errors or omissions brought to their attention so that they may be corrected in subsequent printings.

Weigl acknowledges Getty Images as its primary image supplier for this title.

Contents

Peanuts are a major industry in Alabama. Peanuts grow on plants below ground.

Introduction

A labama is a state of fascinating places and friendly people. The landscape offers a beautiful mix of expansive forests, sandy coastal plains, and bountiful farmlands.

The land has always played an important role in Alabama's economy. The state once depended primarily upon the cotton industry, but over the years, agriculture has expanded into other areas. Today Alabama produces a wide variety of crops, such as soybeans, peanuts, and melons.

Residents and tourists alike enjoy Alabama's more than 20 state parks.

The beaches of the Alabama Gulf Coast attracted more than 4.5 million visitors in 2009.

Industry plays an important role as well. Alabama's abundance of natural resources provides the state with many economic opportunities. The ground yields valuable minerals, while the rivers provide important transportation routes and can be harnessed to produce **hydroelectricity**.

Alabama lies at the southern end of the Appalachian Mountains, which extend down through the northeastern part of the state. The mountains cover nearly half of the state. In the north is the fertile agricultural valley of the Tennessee River. Prairie lowlands south of that area hold rich farmland, where cotton was once the main crop. Farther south stretch huge forests of pine and hardwood trees. While Alabama has only 53 miles of coast, it is famous for white sand beaches.

Where Is Alabama?

Alabama is located in the southeastern United States, also known as the Deep South. It is bordered by Tennessee to the north, Georgia to the east, Florida and the Gulf of Mexico to the south, and Mississippi to the west. The Gulf Coast stretches along the Gulf of Mexico.

The city of Mobile, on the Gulf Coast, is one of the most important **seaports** in the United States. Mobile is located on the Intracoastal Waterway, a 3,000-mile shipping route that connects the Southern states with states along the East Coast.

In World War II, shipyards in Mobile built hundreds of ships for the U.S. Navy. In the 21st century, Mobile's shipyards helped construct the Independence for the U.S. Navy. The Navy tested this warship's seagoing abilities along Mobile's coast.

Alabama was the starting point for both the Civil War and the civil rights movement. The state played a crucial role in the development of the Confederate States of America, formed by the eleven Southern states that **seceded** from the rest of the United States. Montgomery, known as the Cradle of the Confederacy, became the first capital of the Confederacy. In April 1861 in Montgomery, Confederate General P. G. T. Beauregard gave the order to fire on Fort Sumter, a Union fort off the coast of South Carolina. This attack was the first battle in the Civil War between the Confederacy and the Union.

Though the Civil War brought slavery to an end, black Americans continued to suffer from discrimination. In the mid-twentieth century, the civil rights movement in Alabama gained strength as African Americans struggled for freedom and equality. In 1955, Rosa Parks caused a sensation when she refused to give up her seat on a city bus in Montgomery. At the time, Alabama law said that African Americans had to give up their seats to white people. When she was arrested, a local activist, minister Martin Luther King, Jr., led a **boycott** of Montgomery buses. The boycott was one of the first steps on the road to **desegregation** and equal rights for African Americans.

On November 15, 1956, the Supreme Court made segregated seating in buses illegal.

Although Alabama has no official nickname, it is commonly referred to as the Heart of Dixie. It is also sometimes referred to as the Yellowhammer State, which comes from the uniforms worn by Alabama soldiers during the Civil War. The uniforms had yellow trim that resembled the yellow patches on the wings of the yellowhammer bird. Other Alabama nicknames include the Cotton State, the Cotton Plantation State, and the Camellia State.

Alabama's state flag was adopted in 1895. It consists of a crimson cross of St. Andrew on a white background.

The flag of the Confederate States of America was designed in Alabama in 1861.

The Gulf Coast provides a livelihood for the many shrimpers that fish its waters.

Mapping Alabama

Alabama is nearly a square state, with straight lines making up most of its borders. In southeastern Alabama, however, the winding Chattahoochee River forms nearly half of the eastern border. In the northwest tip of the state, the Tennessee River forms a small part of the border. In the southwest, the western edge of the Florida panhandle is not a straight line. The panhandle juts into the state and separates most of southern Alabama from the Gulf of Mexico.

Sites and Symbols

STATE SEAL
Alabama

STATE BIRD
Yellowhammer

STATE FLOWER
Camellia

STATE FLAG
Alabama

STATE MAMMAL
Black Bear

STATE TREE
Southern Pine

Nickname The Heart of Dixie

Motto *Audemus Jura Nostra Defendere* (We Dare Maintain Our Rights)

Song "Alabama," words by Julia S. Tutwiler and music by Edna Gockel Gussen

Entered the Union December 14, 1819, as the 22nd state

Capital Montgomery

Population (2010 Census) 4,779,736 Ranked 23rd state

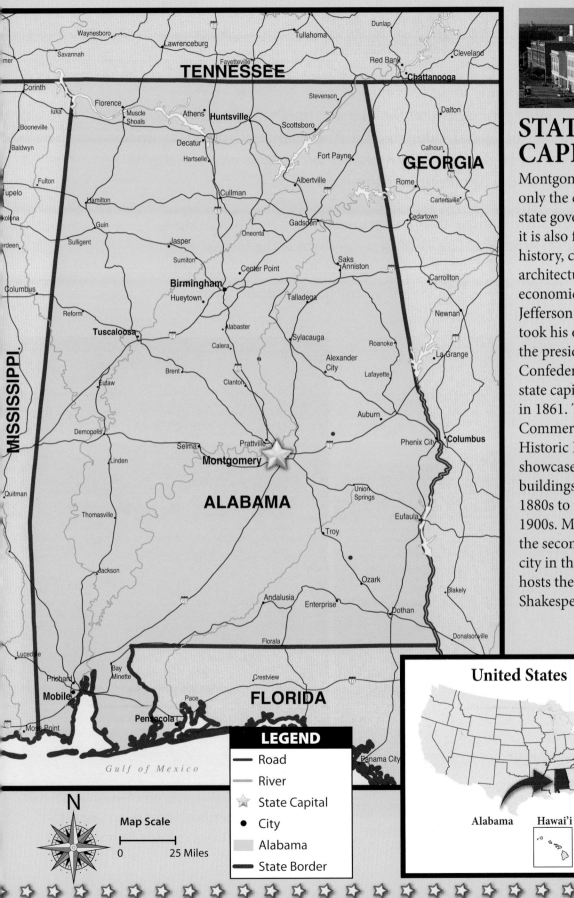

TENNESSEE

Waynesboro
Lawrenceburg
Savannah
mer
Corinth
Iuka
Florence
Muscle Shoals
Athens
Huntsville
Booneville
Baldwyn
Decatur
Hartselle
Tupelo
Fulton
Hamilton
Cullman
okolona
Guin
Sulligent
Jasper
Oneonta
rdeen
Sumiton
Center Point
Columbus
Reform
Birmingham
Hueytown
Tuscaloosa
Alabaster
Calera
Eutaw
Brent
Clanton
Demopolis
Linden
Selma
Prattville
Montgomery
Quitman
Thomasville
ALABAMA
Jackson
Andalusia
Enterprise
Florala
Lucedale
Prichard
Bay Minette
Crestview
Mobile
Pace
FLORIDA
Moss Point
Pensacola
Gulf of Mexico
Panama City

Fayetteville
Tullahoma
Dunlap
Red Bank
Chattanooga
Stevenson
Cleveland
Dalton
Scottsboro
Fort Payne
Calhoun
Albertville
Rome
GEORGIA
Cartersville
Gadsden
Cedartown
Saks
Anniston
Carrollton
Talladega
Newnan
Sylacauga
Roanoke
La Grange
Alexander City
Lafayette
Auburn
Phenix City
Columbus
Union Springs
Eufaula
Troy
Ozark
Blakely
Dothan
Donalsonville

MISSISSIPPI

LEGEND

— Road
— River
⭐ State Capital
● City
▦ Alabama
— State Border

N

Map Scale

0   25 Miles

United States

Alabama   Hawai'i   Alaska

The Land

Alabama is made up of five natural regions. Three of these regions are the Appalachian Plateau, the Piedmont Plateau, and the Ridge and Valley region. Together the three make up the Appalachian Highlands. The Appalachian Plateau includes the southern part of the Appalachian Mountain range.

The Interior Low Plateau, in the northwestern corner of the state, has excellent farmland. The Gulf Coastal Plain is the largest region in Alabama and contains an area called the Black Belt. Named for its fertile soil, the Black Belt is known for its agriculture. The area is also a source of lumber.

CHEAHA MOUNTAIN

The highest point in Alabama is Cheaha Mountain, near Talladega, at 2,407 feet.

APPALACHIAN PLATEAU

With their underground lakes and pools, the Sequoyah Caverns were formed over millions of years.

INTERIOR LOW PLATEAU

The Tennessee River flows through the northern part of Alabama.

GULF COASTAL PLAIN

The Alabama River flows almost completely within the Gulf Coastal Plain.

Huge forests grow in parts of Alabama. Commercial forestland of pine and hardwoods stretches over 22 million acres.

In the Creek Indian language, the word *Alabama* means "tribal town."

Alabama is the thirtieth largest state in the United States.

Tough grasses once thrived among the pine forests of the southeast plains, giving that area the name "the wiregrass section."

The great Onyx Cathedral, in the DeSoto Caverns, is longer than a football field and taller than a 12-story building.

In 2005, Hurricane Katrina shattered beach houses on Dauphin Island and left a path of destruction along the Gulf Coast.

Climate

Alabama has short, mild winters and long, warm summers. Winter temperatures range from 44° to 57° Fahrenheit, while in summer, average temperatures are in the mid-80s. The state receives a considerable amount of rain, and hurricanes occasionally strike the Gulf Coast. Destructive tornadoes sometimes sweep across parts of the state.

The highest temperature ever recorded in Alabama was 112° F, reached on September 5, 1925, in Centerville. On January 30, 1966, Alabama's temperature dipped to its lowest point ever, –27° F at New Market.

Average Annual Precipitation Across Alabama

Cities in different parts of Alabama typically receive different amounts of rainfall over the course of a year. Why might Mobile get the highest amount of precipitation?

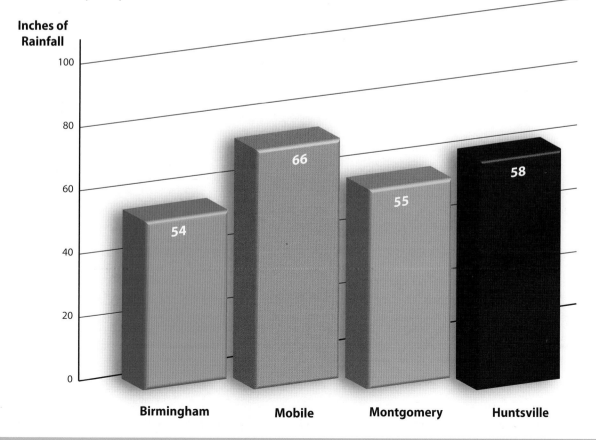

Natural Resources

Alabama has a variety of natural resources. Forests cover about two-thirds of the state. Fertile soils, a long growing season, and abundant rainfall are key to the state's agriculture. Alabama is rich in coal, limestone, **bauxite**, and white marble. The abundance of iron ore, or hematite, has contributed to the successful iron and steel industries in the state. Natural gas is one of the most valuable resources in Alabama. It accounts for more than one-half of the state's income from **fossil fuels**.

Alabama is a major producer of soybeans. Soybeans are used in cooking oil, margarine, shortening, and salad oil as well as in paints, resins, and plastics.

Wilson Dam stretches 4,541 feet across the Tennessee River, producing hydroelectricity and creating Wilson Reservoir. The reservoir is often called the Smallmouth Capital of the World for the many bass caught there.

Alabama's rivers provide water for **irrigation** and recreation. Hydroelectricity is generated at several dams, including Muscle Shoals. The beauty of Alabama's landscape is a valuable resource in and of itself. Wildlife preserves, trees, flowers, and caves help bring billions of tourist dollars into the state each year.

Hematite, a primary source of iron, is the official state mineral of Alabama.

Millions of trees are planted in commercial forests in Alabama each year.

Alabama produces some of the world's finest white marble.

Alabama has 53 miles of coastline.

Alabama's coastal waters are a bountiful resource for the state's fishing industry.

On April 20, 2010, the Deepwater Horizon oil rig exploded, gushing tens of thousands of barrels of oil into the Gulf of Mexico. Oil floated just off the shore of Fort Morgan, threatening the area's wildlife, fishing industry, and tourism.

With its variety of scenery, including the southern end of the Appalachian Mountain chain, Alabama draws hikers to some of the most beautiful woodlands in the South.

Plants

More than 125 species of tree can be found in Alabama. Pine and oak trees grow throughout the state. Black walnut and sweet gum trees are plentiful. Spanish moss grows on many of the state's trees. Alabama has many flowering trees and shrubs, including magnolia, azalea, dogwood, and rhododendron. Common wildflowers, such as thistle, trillium, and prairie clover, add a splash of color to the landscape. Mistletoe, blackberries, huckleberries, and mountain laurels all grow throughout the state.

In 1992, Alabama created the Forever Wild land trust, which is devoted to protecting the state's wildlife. The fund purchases tracts of land that are preserved for outdoor recreation and research.

SPANISH MOSS

Spanish moss often grows on cypress trees and southern live oaks. It looks like a long, silvery beard dripping from tree branches.

TRILLIUM

Trilliums grow in shady woodlands as well as in cultivated wildflower gardens. They are one of the first flowers of spring.

OAK TREES

Live oak trees line the streets of many towns in Alabama. They can grow as tall as 50 feet.

BAMBOO

One of the fastest-growing plants on Earth, bamboo are tall, treelike grasses. Their woody stems can be used for flooring, food, and Chinese medicine.

Alabama's state nut is the pecan. Pecans are often used in Southern cooking.

The four national forests in Alabama are the Bankhead, Conecuh, Tuskegee, and Talladega. They encompass some 665,000 acres.

The Cahaba River is one of the few rivers in Alabama that is not heavily dammed. As a result, it supports a large variety of plant and animal life.

Animals

Alabama's forests contain bobcats, red and gray foxes, raccoons, squirrels, weasels, otters, and opossums. Larger mammals are not as numerous, although there are black bears in the south and white-tailed deer in the west. Bird-watchers keep their eyes open so they won't miss sightings of bald eagles, ospreys, brown pelicans, bluebirds, and great blue herons, among others.

Bass, trout, and catfish swim in Alabama's lakes and rivers. Mullets, red snappers, crabs, oysters, and shrimps live in the waters off the Gulf Coast. Alligators hunt their prey in swamps in the southern region of the state. Thousands of alligators live in the Mobile Delta area. Many poisonous snakes are found in Alabama. These include rattlesnakes, coral snakes, and water moccasins.

BLUE CRAB

Blue crabs live on muddy shores, bays, and estuaries. They can grow to 9 inches long and turn red-orange when cooked.

GREAT HORNED OWL

The great horned owl grows to more than 2 feet long. It feeds on small rodents and birds.

ARMADILLO

The nine-banded armadillo is the only armadillo subspecies in Alabama. Thick scales cover its head and tail, while a shell made of horn and bone protects its back.

AMERICAN ALLIGATOR

The American alligator, the only member of the crocodile family found in Alabama, lives mostly in the freshwater coastal plains. It can tolerate some cold, so it has moved somewhat into Alabama's interior.

Alabama has a state saltwater fish, the fighting tarpon.

There have been very few recorded alligator attacks on people in Alabama.

A very rare animal, the dismalite, lives in Alabama. Dismalites are worms that glow in the dark.

The monarch butterfly is the official insect of Alabama.

Tourism

Tourism is an important business in Alabama. For example, in 2009, nearly 21 million people visited the state and spent more than $9.3 billion. Visitors come to Alabama to enjoy the warm southern climate. Fishing, boating, and other water activities are popular in the state's lakes, rivers, and reservoirs. The Gulf of Mexico is highly regarded as a place for ocean fishing.

The caves and caverns in the northeastern part of Alabama are also popular with tourists. The state has more than 3,000 known caves, making it an ideal spot for **spelunking**. The 14-acre Cathedral Caverns is known for having the world's largest **stalagmite** forest.

UNITED STATES SPACE AND ROCKET CENTER IN HUNTSVILLE

The United States Space and Rocket Center in Huntsville is perhaps the world's largest space-travel attraction. The center has more than 1,500 space artifacts on display and one of NASA's Space Camps. At space camp, children can live like astronauts, experience weightlessness in the Gravity Trainer, eat freeze-dried food, and get the feel for flying in jet-fighter simulators.

McWANE SCIENCE CENTER

The McWane Science Center contains four floors of exhibits, including several on dinosaurs, as well as laser and light exhibits that visitors can experiment with. The aquarium includes a shark and ray touch tank.

BIRMINGHAM ZOO

The Birmingham Zoo was the third most popular tourist attraction in Alabama in 2009.

BIRMINGHAM BOTANICAL GARDENS

The Birmingham Botanical Gardens contain more than 10,000 different plants growing in more than 25 different gardens. Beautiful sculptures dot the grounds.

The skeleton of a prehistoric man was found in a cave at the Russell Cave National Monument.

The Looking Glass Lakes, in the Sequoyah Caverns, are crystal-clear pools that reflect the ceiling of the caverns. The reflected image tricks visitors into thinking that they are looking into a deep gorge rather than a shallow pool of water.

A popular tourist attraction in Mobile is the USS *Alabama*. The ship, used in World War II, is anchored in Mobile Bay and is open to the public.

Industry

Fishing is a multimillion-dollar industry in Alabama. The state has both freshwater and saltwater commercial fishing. Shrimps are the most valuable saltwater seafood. Oysters, blue crabs, and red snappers are also important. Buffalo fish, mussels, and catfish are caught in freshwater streams.

Industries in Alabama
Value of Goods and Services in Millions of Dollars

Alabama is consistently rated as one of the top states where businesses can thrive. It has a good workforce-training program, plenty of natural resources, a good climate for agriculture, and vast forest lands. Health care, however, is predicted to be an area for growing employment over the next two decades. Why do you think that might be?

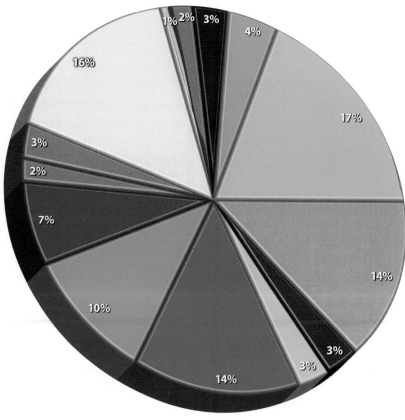

LEGEND

Agriculture, Forestry, and Fishing $2,368
Mining $3,082
Utilities $4,632
Construction $7,568
Manufacturing $29,275
Wholesale and Retail Trade $23,024
Transportation $5,185
Media and Entertainment $5,074
Finance, Insurance, and Real Estate $24,215
Professional and Technical Services $16,191
* Education $799
Health Care $12,272
Hotels and Restaurants $4,189
Other Services $4,388
Government $27,752

TOTAL $170,014

*Less than 1%. Percentages may not add to 100 because of rounding.

Alabama's abundance of mineral resources means that mining is very important to the state's economy. The underground coal mines in western Alabama are some of the deepest in the nation.

The production of iron and steel, in the Birmingham area, is one of the main industries in Alabama. Steel production occurs primarily in Birmingham, Decatur, and Gadsden. **Fabricated metals**, such as cast-iron pipes and metal valves, are also made in the region.

In 2010, a huge new steel plant began operating in northern Alabama, boosting the production of steel in the state.

Alabama is highly ranked in the production of catfish. The catfish are often raised on farms, where farmers flood their croplands to create artificial ponds.

Alabama is one of the largest suppliers of cast-iron and steel-pipe products in the United States.

The Sloss Furnaces in Birmingham were designated a National Historic Site in 1983. The furnaces once employed nearly 500 workers and produced 400 tons of pig, or crude, iron per day.

Alabama is one of the largest producers of **broiler chickens** in the United States.

Goods and Services

Cotton was once Alabama's most important product. The invasion of the **boll weevil** in 1915 destroyed a large proportion of the state's cotton plants, forcing farmers to diversify their crops. Instead of planting only cotton, they began to raise other crops as well. Corn and soybeans are grown in the southern part of Alabama. Peanuts, pecans, hay, oats, tobacco, and wheat are other important crops. The state also produces many fruits and vegetables, including peaches, apples, watermelons, beans, potatoes, and sweet potatoes.

Huntsville is known for its production of missiles. Alabama workers built the rocket that took humans to the Moon. The Marshall Space Flight Center, in Huntsville, is where NASA conducts rocket tests and trains astronauts.

Changes in planting and harvesting machinery allow farmers to reap more cotton from fewer acres.

The pulp and paper industry is another valuable source of income for Alabama. It includes the producers of sanitary paper products, box manufacturers, and pulp and paper mills. Chemical manufacturers in Alabama produce paint, fertilizer, and varnish. **Textile** mills, lumber mills, meatpacking plants, and industrial-machinery factories are also important.

Alabama's waterways help the state transport raw materials and finished products. Ships deliver goods to the state and unload them at the Alabama State Docks in Mobile Bay. The Alabama State Docks operates a system of about 30 general cargo berths and about 4 million square feet of storage space. The ships transport coal, iron, steel, petroleum products, pulp and other wood products, soybeans, and wheat.

The state is home to several major automobile producers, including Mercedes-Benz U.S. International, Honda Manufacturing of Alabama, and Hyundai Motor Manufacturing Alabama.

American Indians

Archaeological sites contain evidence of people living in Alabama as early as 10,000 years ago. These early peoples were hunters who used caves for shelter. By about 1000 BC, they had begun to plant crops and build permanent settlements. Later, they lived in villages built around large mounds of earth. The mounds were an important part of their culture. These early inhabitants are sometimes called the Mound Builders.

One of the largest American Indian settlements in U.S. history was in the area of Moundville Archaeological Park. Begun around 1120, the settlement was a planned development, with housing mounds alternating with burial mounds.

Soon after the time of the Mound Builders, other groups of American Indians began to settle the Alabama area. By the 1700s, four major Indian nations were living in the region. They were the Cherokees, the Creeks, the Choctaws, and the Chickasaws. By the late 1830s, the United States government had forced these groups to move from their homes in Alabama to reservations in Oklahoma to make room for white settlers. Despite the upheaval and deaths caused by these changes, the move west did not extinguish these tribes. All these tribes have thriving cultures today.

Traditional Creek homes were made of dried mud and earth with a thatched grass roof.

Mobile is named after the Mobile, or Maubilia, Indians. This Indian group lived in the area during the early part of the 1700s.

The mounds built by Alabama's early inhabitants stand as high as 60 feet.

During the late 1600s and early 1700s, some Creek and Chickasaw Indians raided Choctaw villages to seize these Indians to sell to British planters as slaves. The British then shipped these Choctaws to the British West Indies to work on sugar plantations.

The Cherokees, Creeks, Choctaws, and Chickasaws brought their religious tradition of stomp dancing when they moved from Alabama to Okalahoma. The dances take place around a sacred fire, with the rhythm provided by women shaking turtle shells attached to their feet.

Late in the 1600s, the Creeks became one of the most powerful groups of American Indian warriors in North America.

One small Creek reservation remains in southern Alabama in Poarch.

Explorers

The first Europeans to reach the Alabama area were Spanish explorers. This group included Alonso Alvarez de Piñeda, who sailed into Mobile Bay in 1519. Around 1540, Spaniard Hernando de Soto and his army moved up from the Gulf of Mexico in search of gold. He raided American Indian villages, took hostages, and tortured Indians for information and for food. De Soto's treatment of American Indians resulted in many conflicts. One of the worst of these battles was with the Indian chief Tuscaloosa at Maubila, or Mobile. The battle resulted in the deaths of several thousand American Indians and left De Soto's troops severely weakened.

Hernando de Soto was already a wealthy man from raiding the Incas in Peru before he began his search for gold in North America.

In 1559, Don Tristán de Luna traveled from Mexico to Mobile, with 500 soldiers and 1,000 colonists, to start a settlement. The group also looked unsuccessfully for gold. In 1561, a fierce storm destroyed much of their food and supplies, forcing them to return to Mexico.

For the next 250 years, the French, British, and Spanish struggled for control of the area. Each group tried to make alliances with American Indian tribes living there.

Timeline of Settlement

Early Exploration

1519 Spanish explorers arrive at what is now Mobile Bay.

1689 French explorers claim for France all the land that was drained by the Mississippi River.

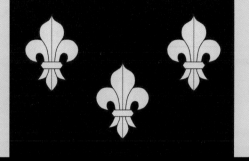

First European Settlements

1702 France founds the first permanent European settlement in Alabama, Fort Louis.

1717 Fort Toulouse is built on the Coosa River to encourage trade with the Indians and reduce the influence of the British.

1763 France **cedes** territorial claims east of the Mississippi River, including Alabama, to Great Britain, as part of the terms to end the French and Indian War.

American Revolution and Civil War

1783 The Treaty of Paris, which formally ends the American Revolution, gives Mobile to Spain and the rest of Alabama to the newly created United States of America.

1813 The United States claims Mobile from Spain.

1819 Alabama becomes the 22nd state.

1830s Creek Indians are illegally removed from their homelands in Alabama and forced to move to Oklahoma.

1861 Alabama secedes from the United States and joins the Confederate States of America.

1868 Alabama ratifies a new state constitution that protects the civil rights of African Americans and is allowed back into the Union as a state.

Early Settlers

I n 1702, French-Canadian explorer Jean-Baptiste Le Moyne, sieur de Bienville, established a French settlement on the Mobile River. After a flood, the settlement was moved to the site of present-day Mobile and renamed Fort Condé de la Mobile. The fort was the center of the French government for the Louisiana colony during the early 1700s.

Map of Settlements and Resources in Early Alabama

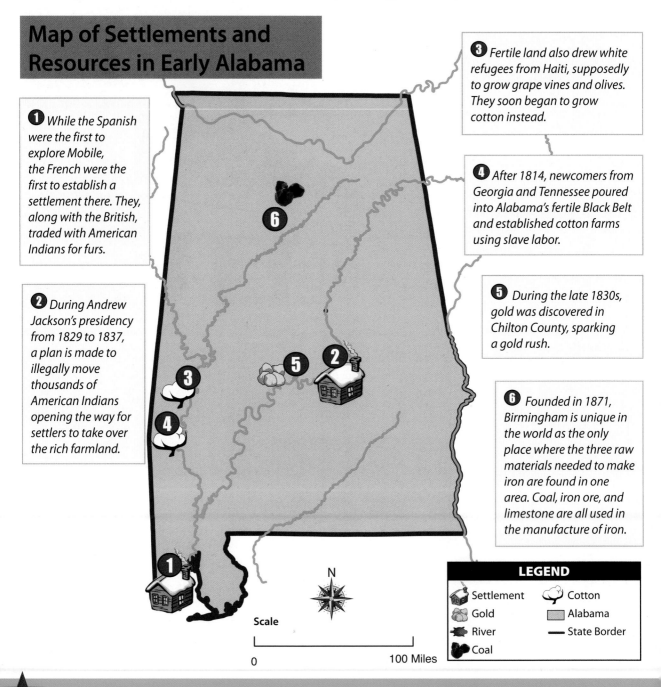

1 While the Spanish were the first to explore Mobile, the French were the first to establish a settlement there. They, along with the British, traded with American Indians for furs.

2 During Andrew Jackson's presidency from 1829 to 1837, a plan is made to illegally move thousands of American Indians opening the way for settlers to take over the rich farmland.

3 Fertile land also drew white refugees from Haiti, supposedly to grow grape vines and olives. They soon began to grow cotton instead.

4 After 1814, newcomers from Georgia and Tennessee poured into Alabama's fertile Black Belt and established cotton farms using slave labor.

5 During the late 1830s, gold was discovered in Chilton County, sparking a gold rush.

6 Founded in 1871, Birmingham is unique in the world as the only place where the three raw materials needed to make iron are found in one area. Coal, iron ore, and limestone are all used in the manufacture of iron.

N

Scale

0

100 Miles

LEGEND

Settlement	Cotton
Gold	Alabama
River	State Border
Coal	

Soon settlers began to arrive from France and Canada. Early French settlers nearly starved to death waiting for supply ships to arrive from France. In 1719, the French brought slaves over from Africa to clear fields and harvest crops.

In 1763, France gave up almost all its territory in North America east of the Mississippi River to Great Britain. When the American Revolution ended in 1783, northern Alabama became part of the United States, while Mobile and southern Alabama were ruled by Spain. The United States seized Mobile from the Spanish, and in 1817, Alabama became a territory of the United States.

Settlers soon moved into the Alabama territory to take advantage of its fertile land. By 1819, enough people lived in the territory to qualify it for statehood. Alabama joined the Union on December 14, 1819.

Beginning in the early 1800s, cotton plantations sprang up across the state. Many thousands of black slaves were forced to work on these plantations.

Notable People

Many notable Alabamans contributed to the development of their state, their nation, and the world. They came from every level of society and every race. These important Alabamans included the original American Indian inhabitants, European American settlers and politicians, and African American activists.

SEQUOYAH
(c. 1760–1843)

Sequoyah was the son of a Cherokee woman and a British trader. He became convinced that developing a system for writing down the oral Cherokee language would help maintain independence from the whites. Because his 86-symbol system was simple, the ability to read and write spread rapidly among the Cherokees, and they were able to publish their own books and newspapers. The giant redwoods of northern California, called the sequoias, are named after him.

GEORGE WASHINGTON CARVER
(1864–1943)

George Washington Carver was the son of slaves. For more than fifty years, he researched agricultural products that revolutionized agriculture in the South. He discovered hundreds of uses for peanuts, soybeans, and sweet potatoes and developed ways to extract dyes from clay soil. In 1896, Carver became the director of the Department of Agricultural Research at Tuskegee Normal and Industrial Institute, now Tuskegee University. His discoveries helped replace cotton as the main agricultural product of Alabama.

HUGO BLACK (1886–1971)

Born in Harlan, Hugo Black spent his early years watching court trials and political rallies, inspiring him to become a lawyer. Once elected to the U.S. Senate, Black introduced minimum-wage legislation, which became law. Appointed to the Supreme Court, he was a strong defender of the right of free speech for everyone.

RALPH DAVID ABERNATHY (1926–1990)

Though the grandchild of a slave, Ralph David Abernathy was raised on his family's large farm in Morengo County. He became a founder of the civil rights movement. Along with Martin Luther King, Jr., he helped lead the Montgomery bus boycott and founded the Southern Christian Leadership Conference, which became the most visible civil rights organization in the South.

CONDALEEZZA RICE (1954–)

Born in Birmingham, Rice showed her intelligence at an early age, graduating from college at age 19. She was also a champion-level ice skater. Originally a college professor and then a policy adviser to government leaders, she became secretary of state for President George W. Bush from 2005 to 2009.

Dr. William Crawford Gorgas (1854–1920) figured out how to control the spread of mosquitoes that cause the disease malaria. His work controlling the insect enabled the United States to complete the Panama Canal by preventing the illness from occurring among the thousands of workers.

Booker T. Washington (1856–1915), the son of a slave, became a well-known educator. He wrote many books, including his **autobiography**, *Up from Slavery*. Washington started the Tuskegee Normal and Industrial Institute, a school for rural African American youths, which later became Tuskegee University.

Population

Nearly 4.8 million people live in Alabama. The five most populous cities in Alabama are Birmingham, Montgomery, Mobile, Huntsville, and Tuscaloosa. According to the 2010 Census, Alabama has a **population density** of more than 94 people per square mile. This is greater than the national average, which is about 87 people per square mile.

According to the U.S. Census Bureau, Alabamians of European heritage made up the largest percentage of the population at 71 percent. African Americans were second at 26 percent.

Alabama Population 1950–2010

Alabama's population has been growing in recent decades, although the rate of growth is not as large as in some other states. Why would people settle in Alabama now?

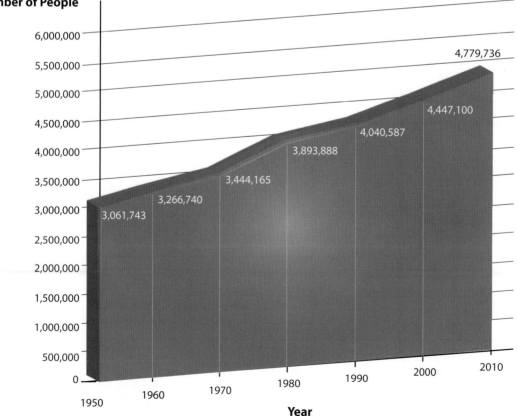

Number of People

- 6,000,000
- 5,500,000 — 4,779,736
- 5,000,000
- 4,500,000 — 4,447,100
- 4,000,000 — 4,040,587
- 3,500,000 — 3,893,888
- 3,444,165
- 3,266,740
- 3,061,743
- 2,500,000
- 2,000,000
- 1,500,000
- 1,000,000
- 500,000
- 0

1950 · 1960 · 1970 · 1980 · 1990 · 2000 · 2010

Year

Birmingham is the largest city in Alabama. The city covers more than 150 square miles.

About 3 percent of Alabamians are Hispanic. Asian Americans and Americans Indians each accounted for less than 1 percent.

Approximately 75 percent of people over the age of 25 in Alabama are high school graduates, while 19 percent have college degrees.

In 2009, Alabama was the ninth poorest state in the nation, with 17 percent of its people living in poverty. However, the number of blacks living in poverty was more than twice the number of whites. The state is working to promote education and jobs for low-income and homeless individuals and families.

Politics and Government

A labama is governed under its sixth constitution, which was adopted in 1901. The Alabama government is divided into three branches. They are the executive, the legislative, and the judicial branches. The governor, who is elected for a four-year term, is the head of the executive branch. The governor's main purpose is to make sure that state laws are enforced. The secretary of state, the state treasurer, and the attorney general are part of the executive branch of government.

The State Capitol in Montgomery, which houses the legislature, was designated a National Historic Site in 1960.

The legislative branch is responsible for creating laws. The Alabama Legislature is made up of a House of Representatives and a Senate. Alabama has 105 state representatives and 35 state senators, all elected for four-year terms.

The judicial branch includes the state Supreme Court, the court of civil appeals, and the court of criminal appeals. All judges and justices are elected for six-year terms.

The Alabama State Board of Education sets standards for schools across the state. The board supports a federal program encouraging former military members to become teachers.

Cultural Groups

Alabama's rich culture has a strong connection to the civil rights movement of the 1950s and 1960s. The Birmingham Civil Rights District serves as an important reminder of the African American struggle for equal rights. The district occupies six city blocks and includes the Birmingham Civil Rights Institute, Kelly Ingram Park, the Carver Theater, and the 16th Street Baptist Church.

Birmingham's Fourth Avenue Business District was a major African American cultural area, similar to the neighborhoods of Harlem in New York City and Bronzeville in Chicago. It was once the location of more than 3,400 African American businesses, some of which still operate today. In the early 1900s, the segregated district was the only place in which African American businesses were permitted to operate. The area thrived with restaurants, financial companies, barbershops, theaters, and nightclubs. Today many of the buildings have been renovated as part of the historic Civil Rights District.

Visitors and residents alike can view the sculptures at Kelly Ingram Park, listen to great jazz musicians at the Alabama Jazz Hall of Fame, or visit with friends in the Fourth Avenue Business District, part of the Birmingham Civil Rights District.

During Mobile's Mardi Gras, masked riders on floats often throw prizes, such as beads, moon pies, doubloons, and candy, to the crowds on the street.

The Birmingham Civil Rights Institute was created in 1992 to educate people about African American culture and the fight for equality. Exhibits show what it was like for African Americans to live in a segregated society, using separate drinking fountains, going to separate schools, and attending civil rights rallies. The institute is a testimony to the struggle for equal services and equal rights.

Alabama's European cultural heritage is celebrated in the city of Mobile. The Mobile **Mardi Gras** is a combination of both French and Spanish traditions. Dozens of groups build elegant floats and parade through downtown Mobile. Mobile's first Mardi Gras parade consisted of one decorated coal wagon hitched up to a mule. Today about 20 separate parades are held over several weeks.

I DIDN'T KNOW THAT!

In May 1963, Kelly Ingram Park, or West Park, was the scene of a clash between civil rights protesters and Birmingham police and firefighters, who made many arrests and turned high-pressure fire hoses on the demonstrators. The civil disobedience had an impact, as Birmingham soon after began to desegregate.

The demonstrations in 1963 resulted in the arrest of civil rights leader Martin Luther King, Jr., who outlined his philosophy of nonviolent protest in "Letter from the Birmingham Jail" while in prison.

In 1963, when the University of Alabama began admitting African American students, there were fears of mob violence. This led U.S. President John F. Kennedy to order the National Guard to escort African American students into the school.

The Birmingham Civil Rights Institute displays a replica of a bus ridden by the **Freedom Riders**.

In 1965, Martin Luther King, Jr., led a second march from Selma to the capitol at Montgomery, but police resistance forced them to turn back.

Arts and Entertainment

Many important scholars and writers have come from Alabama. Helen Keller was an acclaimed author and lecturer from Tuscumbia. Keller, who was blind and deaf, became an inspiration to many by learning, despite her disabilities, to read, using **braille**, and to speak.

Birmingham's Fannie Flagg wrote *Fried Green Tomatoes at the Whistle Stop Cafe*. The novel was made into a film starring Jessica Tandy and Kathy Bates. Alabamian Harper Lee won a Pulitzer Prize for her 1960 novel *To Kill a Mockingbird*. Since its publication, *To Kill a Mockingbird* has never been out of print, and it is one of the most widely read books in the English language.

The American Film Institute has put the movie To Kill a Mockingbird *on its list of 100 greatest movies of all time. Gregory Peck won an Academy Award for his role as lawyer Atticus Finch.*

Traditional music is played throughout Alabama. Jazz, blues, gospel, country, and rock musicians from Alabama are internationally renowned. Many Alabama musicians have been inducted into the Alabama Music Hall of Fame, in Tuscumbia, as well as into the Rock and Roll Hall of Fame and Museum and into the Country Music Hall of Fame, both of which are located outside the state. They include Nat King Cole, Dinah Washington, Tammy Wynette, Hank Williams, Wilson Pickett, and The Temptations.

Hank Williams, sometimes called the Father of Modern Country Music, was born in 1923 in Georgiana. At a time when most other country music singers performed other people's songs, Williams wrote his own music and created his own sound. He was inducted into the Country Music Hall of Fame in 1961. His son and grandson, both also named Hank, extend the family tradition of country music.

Grammy Award–winning singer-songwriter Emmylou Harris was born in Birmingham. Originally known for her country music, she has also recorded in a wide range of musical styles, including folk, rock, and alternative.

Musician and composer Lionel Richie's career began at Tuskegee University with the rhythm and blues group The Commodores. His solo career, begun in 1980, has taken him to international fame.

I DIDN'T KNOW THAT!

Truman Capote grew up in Monroeville. He was the author of such books as *Breakfast at Tiffany's* and *In Cold Blood*. Harper Lee, who knew him as a child, based the character of Dill in *To Kill a Mockingbird* on Capote. *Breakfast at Tiffany's* was made into a successful movie starring Audrey Hepburn.

Before becoming well known as a singer, Alabama's Nat King Cole was a jazz pianist.

Singer Tammy Wynette, known as the First Lady of Country, is from Red Bay. Her song "Stand by Your Man" stood as the bestselling single in country music for 15 years. She was the first female country artist to sell one million records.

Sports

Alabamians love sports. The state has a history of producing world-class athletes. University football teams have a large and enthusiastic following. The teams in the state, such as the University of Alabama's Crimson Tide and Auburn University's Auburn Tigers, share intense rivalries. Famous National Football League players from Alabama include Bart Starr, Joe Namath, and Ken Stabler.

Avid golfers travel to Alabama to play the 468-hole Robert Trent Jones Golf Trail. The trail includes golf courses at 11 different locations across the state. Outdoor recreation can also be found in Alabama's 22 state parks. Families go to the parks for swimming, hiking, fishing, boating, and camping.

Forward Mia Hamm led three U.S. teams to Olympic medals during her career in soccer.

Slugger Hank Aaron led the National League in home runs in four seasons during his career.

In baseball, Alabama produces home run hitters. Baseball legend Hank Aaron was born in Mobile in 1934. He was a professional baseball player for 23 seasons, during which he hit an amazing total of 755 home runs. He is also known for his quiet fight against discrimination in professional baseball. Born in Westfield in 1931, Willie Mays was the star center fielder for the Giants for most of his career and hit 660 home runs. Aaron and Mays are among the top home run hitters in the history of Major League Baseball.

Track and field star Jesse Owens was born in Oakville in 1913. He began to set world track and field records when he was still in high school. At the 1936 Olympic Games in Berlin, Germany, Owens won gold medals in the 100-meter dash, 200-meter dash, long jump, and 400-meter relay. At the time, German leader Adolf Hitler was claiming the racist theory that all nonwhite, non-European peoples were inferior. By winning his four gold medals, Owens proved him wrong.

Jesse Owens' outstanding performance in track and field at the 1936 Olympics made him a national hero in the United States.

I DIDN'T KNOW THAT!

Charles Barkley, one of the National Basketball Association's fifty greatest players, was born in Leeds and attended Auburn University.

The Alabama Sports Hall of Fame, established in 1967, honors and highlights the contributions that athletes have made to the state.

Track star Carl Lewis, who won nine Olympic gold medals, was born in Birmingham in 1961.

The Birmingham Black Barons were one of the best-known baseball teams in the Negro Leagues, a segregated African American league in the first half of the 20th century.

Boxer Joe Louis was born in Lafayette in 1914. His 12-year reign as heavyweight boxing champion is the longest ever.

National Averages Comparison

The United States is a federal republic, consisting of fifty states and the District of Columbia. Alaska and Hawai'i are the only non-contiguous, or non-touching, states in the nation. Today, the United States of America is the third-largest country in the world in population. The United States Census Bureau takes a census, or count of all the people, every ten years. It also regularly collects other kinds of data about the population and the economy. How does Alabama compare to the national average?

Comparison Chart

United States 2010 Census Data *	USA	Alabama
Admission to Union	NA	December 14, 1819
Land Area (in square miles)	3,537,438.44	50,744.00
Population Total	308,745,538	4,779,736
Population Density (people per square mile)	87.28	94.19
Population Percentage Change (April 1, 2000, to April 1, 2010)	9.7%	7.5%
White Persons (percent)	72.4%	68.5%
Black Persons (percent)	12.6%	26.2%
American Indian and Alaska Native Persons (percent)	0.9%	0.6%
Asian Persons (percent)	4.8%	1.1%
Native Hawaiian and Other Pacific Islander Persons (percent)	0.2%	0.1%
Some Other Race (percent)	6.2%	2.0%
Persons Reporting Two or More Races (percent)	2.9%	1.5%
Persons of Hispanic or Latino Origin (percent)	16.3%	3.9%
Not of Hispanic or Latino Origin (percent)	83.7%	96.1%
Median Household Income	$52,029	$42,586
Percentage of People Age 25 or Over Who Have Graduated from High School	80.4%	75.3%

*All figures are based on the 2010 United States Census, with the exception of the last two items.

How to Improve My Community

Strong communities make strong states. Think about what features are important in your community. What do you value? Education? Health? Forests? Safety? Beautiful spaces? Government works to help citizens create ideal living conditions that are fair to all by providing services in communities. Consider what changes you could make in your community. How would they improve your state as a whole? Using this concept web as a guide, write a report that outlines the features you think are most important in your community and what improvements could be made. A strong state needs strong communities.

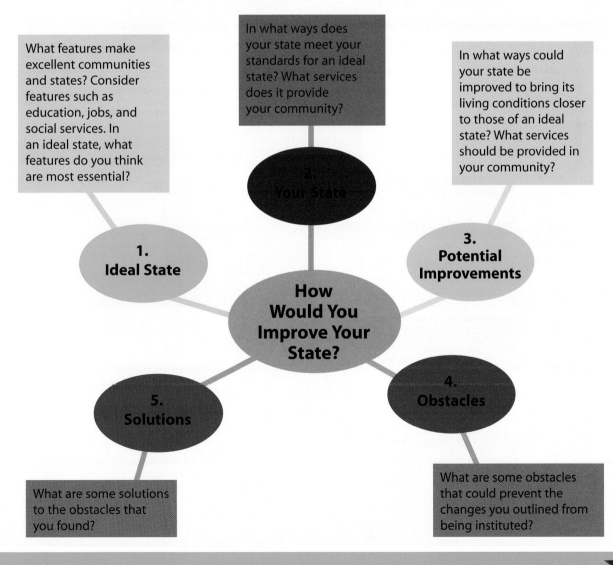

What features make excellent communities and states? Consider features such as education, jobs, and social services. In an ideal state, what features do you think are most essential?

In what ways does your state meet your standards for an ideal state? What services does it provide your community?

In what ways could your state be improved to bring its living conditions closer to those of an ideal state? What services should be provided in your community?

2.
Your State

1.
Ideal State

3.
Potential Improvements

How Would You Improve Your State?

4.
Obstacles

5.
Solutions

What are some solutions to the obstacles that you found?

What are some obstacles that could prevent the changes you outlined from being instituted?

Think about these questions and then use your research skills to find the answers and learn more fascinating facts about Alabama. A teacher, librarian, or parent may be able to help you locate the best sources to use in your research.

1 Which of the following athletes was not born in Alabama?

a. Carl Lewis
b. Ty Cobb
c. Joe Louis
d. Willie Mays

2 Which Alabama city is known as the Rocket Capital of the World?

a. Montgomery
b. Mobile
c. Huntsville
d. Birmingham

3 What is Alabamian George Washington Carver considered by many to be?

4 What new system of transportation was built in Montgomery in 1886?

5 Which well-known basketball star played baseball for the Birmingham Barons?

6 Where does the name *Alabama* come from?

7 Which body of water was the first in the New World to be accurately charted?

8 In what year did Alabama's first school open?

Words to Know

archaeological: related to the study of early peoples through artifacts and remains

autobiography: the story of a person's own life written by that person

bauxite: a clay-like rock that is the main ore in aluminum

boll weevil: a small beetle that feeds on cotton bolls

boycott: a refusal to purchase or participate in something as a means of protest

braille: a method of writing for the blind that uses a system of raised dots on the page

broiler chickens: chickens raised for their meat rather than their eggs

cedes: yields or grants something, usually by treaty

desegregation: the ending of legal separations and restrictions based on race

fabricated metals: metals that are manufactured

fossil fuels: fuels made from fossils, such as oil, coal, and natural gas

Freedom Riders: people who traveled in buses across the South in 1961 to protest segregation, the forced separation of races and restrictions based on race

hydroelectricity: electricity produced using moving water

irrigation: the supplying of water to fields by means of a system of pipes, ditches, or streams

Mardi Gras: a festival whose name means "Fat Tuesday" in French, celebrated on the final Tuesday before Christian Lent

population density: the average number of people per unit of area

seaports: harbor towns or cities from which ships can drop off or pick up cargo

seceded: formally left an organization or nation

spelunking: the recreational activity of exploring caves and caverns underground

stalagmite: a cone-shaped stone formation on the floors of caves

textile: a fabric made by weaving or knitting

Index

Log on to www.av2books.com

AV² by Weigl brings you media enhanced books that support active learning. Go to www.av2books.com, and enter the special code found on page 2 of this book. You will gain access to enriched and enhanced content that supplements and complements this book. Content includes video, audio, web links, quizzes, a slide show, and activities.

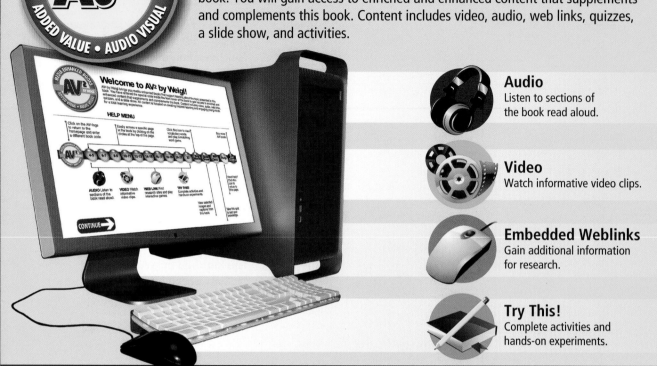

Audio
Listen to sections of the book read aloud.

Video
Watch informative video clips.

Embedded Weblinks
Gain additional information for research.

Try This!
Complete activities and hands-on experiments.

WHAT'S ONLINE?

Try This!	Embedded Weblinks	Video	EXTRA FEATURES
Test your knowledge of the state in a mapping activity.	Discover more attractions in Alabama.	Watch a video introduction to Alabama.	**Audio** Listen to sections of the book read aloud.
Find out more about precipitation in your city.	Learn more about the history of the state.	Watch a video about the features of the state.	**Key Words** Study vocabulary, and complete a matching word activity.
Plan what attractions you would like to visit in the state.	Learn the full lyrics of the state song.		
Learn more about the early natural resources of the state.			**Slide Show** View images and captions, and prepare a presentation
Write a biography about a notable resident of Alabama.			
Complete an educational census activity.			**Quizzes** Test your knowledge.

AV² was built to bridge the gap between print and digital. We encourage you to tell us what you like and what you want to see in the future.
Sign up to be an AV² Ambassador at www.av2books.com/ambassador.